SCHOLASTIC

Phonics

You Cannot Fool Me

Published in the UK by Scholastic Education, 2022
Scholastic Distribution Centre, Bosworth Avenue, Tournament Fields, Warwick, CV34 6UQ
Scholastic Ireland, 89E Lagan Road, Dublin Industrial Estate, Glasnevin, Dublin, D11 HP5F

SCHOLASTIC and associated logos are trademarks and/or registered trademarks of Scholastic Inc.
www.scholastic.co.uk
© 2022 Scholastic Limited
1 2 3 4 5 6 7 8 9   2 3 4 5 6 7 8 9 0 1

Printed by Ashford Colour Press
The book is made of materials from well-managed, FSC-certified forests
and other controlled sources.

A CIP catalogue record for this book is available from the British Library.

ISBN 978-0702-30895-6

Author
Charlotte Raby
Editorial team
Rachel Morgan, Vicki Yates, Tracy Kewley, Jennie Clifford
Design team
Dipa Mistry, Justin Hoffmann, Andrea Lewis, We Are Grace
Illustrations
Camilla Gallindo/Beehive Illustration

Help your child to read!

This book practises these letters and letter sounds.
Point and say the sounds with your child:

ai **ee** **oo (as in 'fool')**

Your child may need help to read these common tricky words:

you **me** **are** **sure** **the** **no** **and**

Before reading
- Look at the cover picture and read the title together. Read the back cover blurb to your child.
- Ask your child: *Have you ever played a funny trick on anyone? What happened?*

During reading
- If your child gets stuck on a word, remind them to sound it out and then blend the sounds to read the word: h-oo-t-s, hoots.
- If they are still stuck, show them how to read the word.
- Enjoy looking at the pictures together. Pause to talk about the story.

After reading
- Ask your child: *Do toads really moo?* Look it up. The bullfrog really does make a sound similar to a cow's moo!

Can you spot the duck on 6 pages?

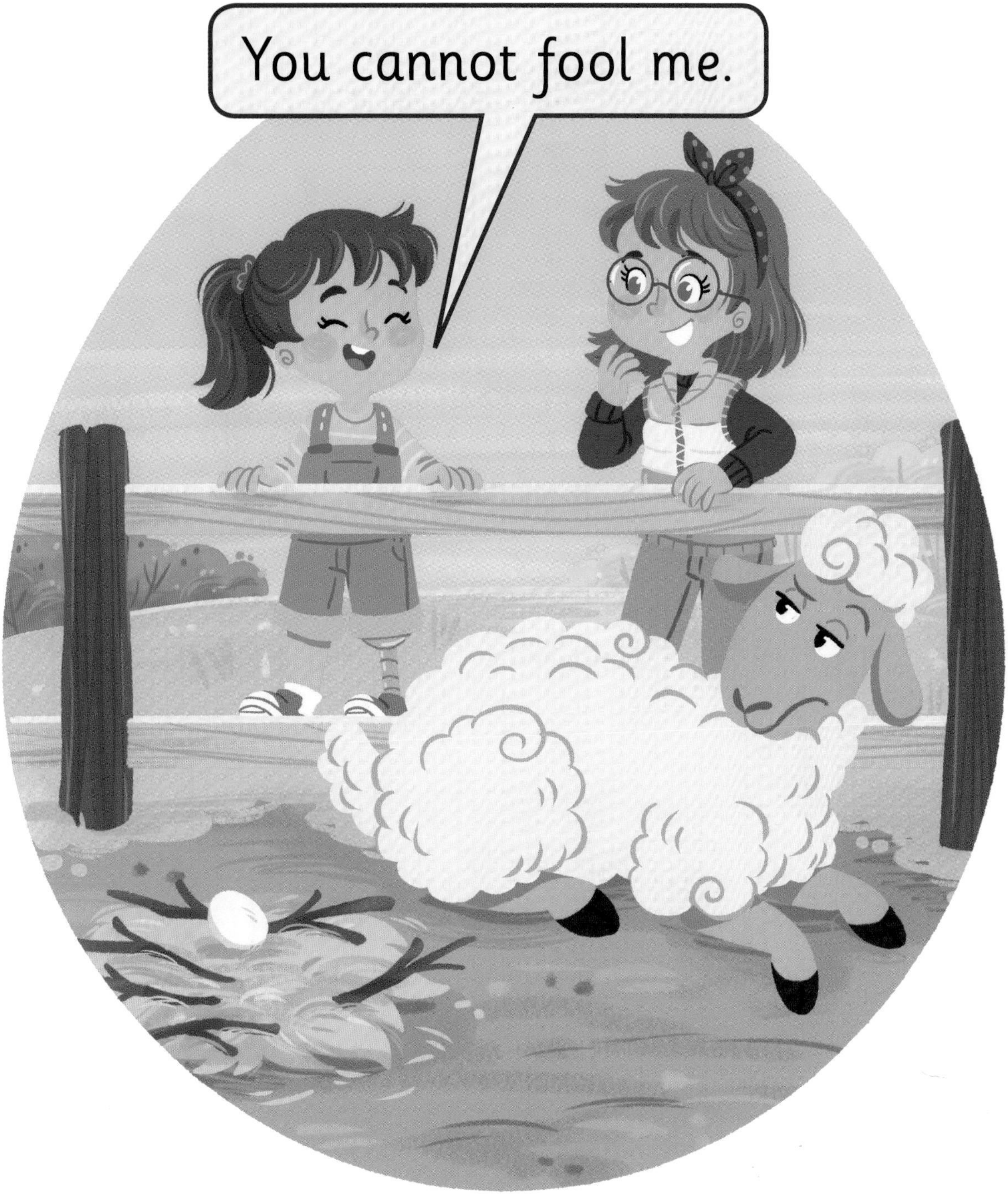
You cannot fool me.

This chicken hoots at night.

This bee moos at the moon.

No! You cannot fool me.

The chicken laid the egg, not the sheep, and...

Retell the story